WHY TITHE

YOUR KEY TO FINANCIAL DOOR

By Pastor Cecilia Mwangi Thuita

Unless otherwise indicated, all scripture Quotations are taken from New King James Version(NKJV)

Published by:
Pastor Cecilia Mwangi
Tel: +1 (510) 600-8865
Email: mwangicecilia72@gmail.com

PREFACE:

WHAT IS TITHE?

Tithe is a tenth of your income or substance (all your possessions/ properties) which belongs to God and should be given to Him faithfully. Most Christians label it Old Testament law and that we're living during the dispensation of grace where the law has no effect.

Partly true, we live in the dispensation of grace but the word of GOD and its instruction haven't changed. "And all the tithe of the land, whether of the seed of the land or of the fruit of the tree, is the LORD'S it is Holy unto the Lord. And if a man will redeem any of his tithes, he shall add to it the fifth part thereof. And concerning the tithe of the herd, or of the frock, even if whatsoever passes under the rod, the **tenth** shall be holy to the Lord." Leviticus 27:30-32.

Misunderstanding of the absolute importance of the tithing and its preferred status have robbed Christians of right standing before God, and it's important to mention here that this requirement was there before the law; in the time of Abraham, when he gave a tenth of his loot to Melchizedek.

Tithe is an obligation for all believers (Christians).

It is God's way of supporting the ministry and believers must support God in doing so. You are to pay your tithe in the house of God. Numbers 18:20-21. "And the Lord spoke to Aaron, You shall have no inheritance in their land, neither shall you have any part among them: I am your part and your inheritance among the children of Israel. And behold, I have given the children of Levi all tenth in Israel for inheritance, for their service of the tabernacle of the congregation."

In the New Testament Matthew 23:23, "Woe unto you, Scribes and Pharisees, hypocrites! For you pay tithe of mint and anise and cumin, and have omitted the weightier matters of the law, justice, mercy and faith: these ought you to have done, and not to leave the other undone."

Jesus was talking of Pharisees as hypocrites who obeyed the letter of the law but not the spirit of the law. Malachi is a Hebrew name meaning messenger or 'my angel'. This is one of the twelve minor prophets of the Old Testament.

Malachi 3:6-12; "For am the Lord, I change not; therefore you sons of Jacob are not consumed. Even from the days of your fathers you have gone away from my ordinances, and have not kept them. Return unto me,

 and I will return unto you, says the Lord of hosts, but you say, How shall we return? Will a man rob God? Yet you have robbed me. But, you say, "How have we robbed you? In tithes and offerings." You are cursed with a curse: for you have robbed me, even this whole nation.

Bring you all the tithes into the storehouse, that there may be food in my house, and test me now in this, says the Lord of hosts. If I will not open you the windows of heaven, and pour you out a blessing, that there shall not be room enough to receive it. And I will rebuke the devourer for your sakes, and he shall not destroy the fruits of your ground: neither shall your vine cast its fruit before the time in the field, said the Lord of hosts. And all the nations shall call you blessed for you shall be a delightful land, says the Lord of hosts."

Table of Contents

INTRODUCTION:
PRINCIPLES OF TITHING:

(a) The Lord makes it clear he's robbed by men when we withhold our tithes and offerings. It's an expression of astonishment. "Will a man rob God?" It's astonishing because it is such an adoring thing to do, shamefully ungrateful, senselessly, self-destructive, because it will certainly be punished.

(b) God calls it robbery because they had unlawful possession of what belonged to God and him only. Tithe belongs to God and Him alone.

(c) If you give 10% of your income or assets to God, the rest also belongs to him 90% but he entrusts it to you to directly manage on his behalf.

(d) The law of masses had a detailed system of giving based on the tithe but if you failed to pay you were assessed a penalty. Leviticus 20.

…You are cursed with a curse, for you have robbed me. This happens because God's people did not give as he commands. God did not bless them materially or spiritually the way he would have otherwise the stingy hearts proved that their hearts were far from God as he is the greatest giver. John 3:16. "For God so loved the world that he gave his only begotten son, that whosoever believes in him should not perish,

but have an everlasting life."

Many of us with financial problems fail to do the most important thing, to obey and honor God with our resources. "When we put God and his Kingdom first he promises to meet our other needs. Matthew 6:33; "But seek you first the Kingdom of God and his righteousness; and all these things shall be added on to you."

Malachi 3:10, "Bring all the tithes into the storehouse…" This was the answer to their problems to actually do what God commanded them to do. This does not mean they were not giving but not everything that God asked for.

We should give with a good attitude like early Christians, who essentially said, 'we are not under the tithe, we can give more!' Giving and financial management are spiritual issues not just a financial issue. Luke 16:11; "And if you are untrustworthy about worldly wealth, who will trust you with the riches of heaven?"

…that there may be food in my house:

The purpose of the tithes was primarily to support the priests who ministered before God. When the people did not bring their tithes, the priests were not properly

supported and there was not enough food for them in the house of the Lord.

Tithe was set aside to support the tribe of Levi and the priests which is the case even today.

...And try (test) me now on this:

It's hard to find a comparable passage of scripture, where the Lord commands his people to test him, and see his faithfulness in keeping his part of his promise in regard to blessing his people who would keep his word by doing what he has asked of them. This shows God is very serious about this teaching of tithing and he is faithful.

...Open for you the windows of heaven and pour out for you such a blessing that there will not be room enough to receive it.

The reference to the windows of heaven reminds of the glorious account of provision for example 2 Kings 7:18-20, when Elisha said and it came to pass as the man of God spoke to the King, saying "Two measures of barley for a Shekel, and a measure of his flour for a

Shekel, shall be tomorrow about this time in the gate of Samaria.

And the Lord answered the man of God, and said, Now; behold if the Lord should make windows in heaven, might such a thing be? And he said, Behold you shall see it with your eyes, but shall not eat of it. And so it happened unto him, for people trod upon him in the gate, and died."

This shows that God can provide in a completely unexpected way! God has resources that we know nothing about; and it is often no help to try or worry about how He can provide. So it is good to serve God with our tithes trusting for his provision as God is faithful to his covenant promises.

…And I will rebuke the devourer

So that the labor of man should not perish, God will give you his token pleasure. The notable thing about this entire description of the manifestation of God's favor is that only the blessings mentioned are of material character. It would seem that God decided to meet the people on their own level.(Prosperity is the key here).

Devourer cannot be stopped or rebuked by prayers or annointing as they have legal rights to stay and scatter as long as God does not protect you. Only when you are faithful in tithing God rebuke devourer out of your

life and you begin to prosper. Conditional blessings have certain conditions attached to them and if you meet, the blessings are no longer available.

CHAPTER ONE

DANGERS OF NOT TITHING:

(a) If you don't tithe, God himself curses you, not the devil and it's only you who can redeem yourself by doing what is required of you by God.

(b) It is impossible for God to put you in stewardship of his finances and wealth if you are not faithful to him in money matters. When God curses, no man can bless. The person has the key for his or her financial breakthrough.

(c) God will not trust you with his power anointing and other spiritual potential if he sees that you are not faithful, with simple material things.

(d) Many prayers have not been assured due to lack of tithing because we learn that tithing is paying back to God;

(e) By not tithing in essence means; you ate the holy things and by doing so, dethroned God from his throne and imposing yourself as god and there after returning to him his throne back. The bible says, our God is a jealous God who:

If we don't pay tithe for the priests to use,

they will neglect God's work. They will be burdened by their own pressure and have little time for people. (God has thus set order in that minister to us spiritually while we minister to them physically by paying our tithes). Hebrews 7:5- "And verily they that are of the sons of Levi, who receive the office of the priesthood, have a commandment to take tithes of the people according to the law, that is of their brethren, though they are descendants of Abraham".

God does not rebuke the devourer on your behalf. 1 John 5:14 "This is the confidence that we have in Him; if we ask anything according to His will, He hears us. And if we know that he hears us; whatever we ask we know that we have petitions that we have asked".

CHAPTER TWO

BENEFITS OF TITHING:
Tithing releases self-confidence to approach God.

❖ Tithes create a divine partnership that makes God involved in every future event of your life. If you have more than you can prioritize, organize or supervise, you have got more than you really deserve.

❖ Tithing plants the seed of expectation in your subconscious mind. You are one continuous seed

❖ saving system (creating atmosphere for reaction) because we are walking magnets expecting response.

❖ It helps us to be disciplined to put God first. Matthew 6:33.

❖ Your money is under the umbrella of God's blessing (God's covering)

❖ You have a covenant with God and nobody can break it. 90% is secured by your 10%.

❖ You live in supernatural blessings not with your own ability or currency flow.

❖ When you tithe, an expectation becomes alive in you. Your expectation is from a qualified source capable of responding to you away from pain to gain.

❖ Tithe unleashes this dormant suffocating force called expectation proof everything in their being able to perform at its highest level because of the expectation.

❖ Expectation energizes you to pursue uncommon miracles. Mark 5:29; "When she had heard of Jesus, came in the crowd behind and touched his garment, Vse 28, for she said, if I may touch but his clothes, I shall be made whole. And immediately the fountain of her blood was dried up; and she felt in her body that she was healed of her disease".

❖ Expectation attracts the right people to you and silences voices of doubt in your life and starts walking in confidence.

❖ You will only achieve uncommon dreams and goals if you fuel and work with force of expectation inside of your life.

❖ Tithing immediately qualifies you to receive the anointing that flows through that house of God that you tithe. Numbers 11:17; "And I will come down and talk with you there: and I will take some of the spirit which is upon them and they shall bear the burden of the people with you, that you bear it not yourself alone". The anointing you respect is the anointing that increases in your life.

❖ Tithing instantly erases all consequences of past greed, past theft and past ignorance that all the history of your past mistakes. Lamentations 3:22,23; "It's of the Lord's mercies that we are not consumed, because his compassion fail not, they are new every morning great is his faithfulness".

❖ Tithing authorizes God to confront on your behalf your adversaries he says he will rebuke your devourer for your sake. Malachi 3:11. So our part is to stay partners for what we do not know he knows it all.

❖ It also memorizes the demons assigned to stop you and it makes Satan lose hope with you because he knows the reward of obedience is yours.

CHAPTER THREE

WHERE TO TITHE:

Know the right mountain, your local church where you are fed spiritually Matt 3:10 in store house.. So be in the right church with God's priests.

You should tithe immediately according to your weekly, monthly income payment so to keep comment flow.

Tithe from gross not net.

LACK OF TITHING

Through the prophet Malachi, God first of all asks the question: **"Will a man rob God?"** To make sure they got the answer right, He answers His own question: **"...you rob me...in** *tithes* and *offerings"* (Mal. 3:8).

The Jews then, were guilty of" doubly robbing" God! They were guilty on two Accounts. They were **"robbing God"** by *withholding* both their **"tithes"** and their **"Offerings."** Theirs was the *sin of* omission – or *withholding from God* what He rightly deserved. The **"tithe"** meant a *tenth* of their income. The **"offering"** meant the various *"animal sacrifices"... "Grain offerings"... drink libations"* they were not bringing into God's storehouse. Further, these **"offerings"** refer to the *"sin offering," "burnt offering"* and *"fellowship offering"* – or *"peace offering"* – they were supposed to regularly

17

bring to God at the Temple. Note a few selective verses about what God instructed them about tithing.

· **"A *tithe of everything* from the land, whether grain from the soil or fruit from the trees, belongs to the Lord; it is *holy* to the Lord"** (Lev. 27:30).

· **"You must...seek the place the Lord your God will choose. To put His Name...To that place you must go; there bring your *burnt offerings* and *sacrifices,* your *tithes* and *special gifts*...your *freewill offerings,* and the *firstborn of your herds and flocks"* (Deut. 12:46).

· *"Be sure to set aside a tenth of all that your fields produce each year...so that you may learn to revere the Lord your God always"* (Deut. 14:23)*"But WHY,"* we *may ask, "did God require these "tithes and offerings"* in the first* place? What was their purpose? *Did God need their money?* Did He love the savory aroma of meat burning on the altar — like we love the smell of a good steak cooking on our backyard grill?" Hardly!

God needs nothing. He is the only complete, all sufficient being in the universe. He is *God —* which is exactly what the **"tithes and offerings"** were to symbolize. They were reminders that God alone is God — and deserving of our love and adoration. Simply put then, these various **"tithes and offerings"** were for the *worship of God,* and the *work of God.*

First and foremost, the *tithe* was a vital part of the *worship of God.* The giving of the *tenth* was a reminder that God was the **"Creator"** of everything. As such, He alone is the **"Possessor of heaven and earth"** (Gen. 14:19; Ps. 24:1). Man was created as the *proprietor* of God's creation – not the *possessor* (Gen. 1:28). The man and woman were but *workers* in His vineyard – not the *owners*. They were dependent *stewards* while God alone was *sovereign*.

So the *tithe* was an outward expression of their *reverence* of God as *God*. They must never entertain the thought that they were totally self-sufficient like God – and could be their own gods. He alone was God and they were not – and the giving of the *tithe* was a material demonstration of that fact. That is because the *"lesser"* gives to the *"greater"* – just as Abraham did to Melchizedek, who in turn **"...blessed Abram"** (Gen.14:1820;Heb. 7:7). So *when man tithes – God blesses*. It's that simple!

Therefore, the *tithe* was a physical, visible, material symbol of the people's *humility* and *reverence* before God. Note again this verse we looked at earlier:
"Be sure to set aside a *tenth* of all that your fields produce each year...so that you may learn to *revere* the Lord your God always" (Deut. 14:2223; Mal. 2:5; Ps. 22:23; 33:8).
So the tithe was to teach them to *revere* and *respect* the Lord as God. The **"tithes and offerings"** were also

"visual aids" to *teach their children* to love and revere God (Ex. 12:2527;
Deut. 4:910). As the children watched their parents give their **"tithes and offerings,"** it taught them to do the same. It built the *principle of submission* and the *principle of giving* into their lives.

Secondly, the tithe was for the support of the workers of God. Since God did not give the Levites any of the Promised Land whereby they could support themselves – He supported them through the tithe: "**The Lord said to Aaron, 'You will have no inheritance in their land, nor will you have any share among them; I am your share and your inheritance among the Israelites. I give to the Levites all the tithes in Israel as their inheritance in return for the work they do while serving at the Tent of Meeting'"** (Num.18:2021; Lev. 27:30, 33;Heb. 7:5).

CHAPTER FOUR

In **Malachi 3:7-12,** I have learned great steps to financial freedom and blessing rooted in the practice of tithing.

1. Review your faithfulness

2. Release your funds

 3. Receive your fruitfulness.

"Ever since the time of your forefathers you have turned away from my decrees and have not kept them. Return unto me and I will return to you" says the Lord Almighty. *"But you ask, 'how are we to return?' "Will a man rob God? "Yet you rob me. "But you ask 'how do we rob you?' "In tithes and offerings" You are under a curse-the whole nation of you- because you are robbing me. Bring the whole tithe into the storehouse, that there may be food in my house. Test me in this"* says the Lord Almighty. *"And see if I will not throw open the floodgates of heaven and pour out so much blessing that you will not have room enough for it. I will prevent the pests (devourer) from devouring your crops and the vines in your fields will not cast their fruit"* says the Lord Almighty. *"Then all the nations will*

call you blessed for yours will be a delightful land" says the Lord Almighty. **Malachi 3:7-12**

Step One: Review your faithfulness.

Malachi begins by asking us to review our faithfulness to God in terms of our finances. God takes up a voice of complaint and rebuke in doing so saying, since the days of their forefathers they have gone against God's decrees and have not kept them. For their sake God initiates a suit. *"Return to me and I will return to you"* **says the Lord Almighty.** *But you ask 'how are we to return to you?'* In this suit the Lord lays three aspects of the problem of our possible lack of faithfulness in our finances.

Resistance – For the Lord says that from the days of your fathers you have resisted God's decrees. Note here in this passage God is not dealing with finances. The obedience of tithing is part of a large picture of overall obedience. God is after our hearts not our wallets. **"I want you"** says the Lord. And so he adds **Return to me!**

There were other issues that God rebukes them for. They gave a half-hearted worship and dishonored God's Name. The Priests were not instructing the people and giving good example, men dealt treacherously with their wives through divorce, that the people considered the Lord's way tedious, and that they exalted the arrogant and the evil doer. And yes! They did not bring their tithes to the storehouse of God. So there is an overall resistance to God's will of which the refusal to return one tenth of their income to God was one part. God does not hesitate to call withholding of tithes in its Proper name **Robbery.**

Robbery –God says *"will a man rob God? Yet you have robbed me. But you say wherein have we robbed you? And God responds "In tithes and offerings"* Robbery? Is this not a very strong language! The first tenth of all things belongs to God and to take it, withhold or keep what belongs to another without consent is robbery. **(Leviticus 27:30; Deuteronomy 12:11; 14:22; Proverbs 2:9, 10; Matthew 23:23).** Looking through the scripture it is clear that Abraham commenced it, Jacob continued it, and Moses commanded it, Jesus commended it. So why resist it?

Results-Where there is lack of faithfulness and obedience God announces the results. *"You are cursed with a curse: for you have robbed me, even this whole nation"* It's absurd to expect blessing from God when we disobey Him. **Galatians 6:7** still stands *"whatever one sows that he will reap"* Jesus said *"If then you are not faithful in the unrighteous mammon, who will entrust you true riches? And if you are not faithful in that which is another's who will give you that which is yours"* **(Lk.16:11-12).** If God cannot trust you with ten shillings why should He trust you with greater things? Thus the curse comes in terms of meager harvest. Since we cannot be trusted with little, He certainly cannot trust us with more. Hence we are cursed with lack of resources due to our own untrustworthiness.

Step Two: Release your funds.

The text Malachi 3:10 say *"bring all the tithes into the storehouse, that there may be food in my house"*. God sets a definite proportion to be brought into the designated place for a definite purpose.

Definite proportion- *"Bring all the tithes"* The tithe is the first tenth of all income. This is different from giving the left-over. This is a deliberate, purposeful giving. Some people ask 'do I give the tithe from the gross or from the net of my income?' If it is the first tenth of your income it must be from the gross not from the net.

Designated place- *"Into the storehouse"* In the Temple was a storehouse. Thus the designated place was the Temple. Today your designated place is where you are fed spiritually. This will be discussed in great details later in the book. Your church is your storehouse.

Determined purpose- *"that there may be food in my house"* in other words that there may be a wherewithal to do God's work. Churches operate on budgets that cater for salaries of Church workers, projects and programs that enable the kingdom of God to expand. Without resources the Church will not accomplish its Mission of reconciling the world back to God. God will not be out done in generosity. If we are faithful in our finances, God will release a blessing.

Step Three- Receive your Fruitfulness.

The Lord says try me in this and see I will open the windows of heaven and pour blessings; I will rebuke the devourer for your sakes. Then the nations will call you blessed for you will be a land of delight. This announces a fourfold blessing to those who are faithful in their tithing.

Renew Your Faith -"*Prove me now herewith or try me in this says the Lord*"

When you get right with God in your finances you will find your faith strengthened. How is that? In the laboratory of our own life, it shall be clear that God is faithful to his promises. **Prov.11:24-25** *"There is one* who holds yet lives in want and there is one who scatters yet increases the more" This is the only text in the whole Bible that God allows or calls us to try him. Otherwise it's clear from the Ten Commandments that you shall not try the Lord your God. Try Him in your tithes and see what He can do.

Return your Fortune: The Lord says *"I will open the windows of heaven and pour blessing that there shall not be room enough to receive it."* The fearful say if I tithe I will have less. No! Says God *"you will have more"* Another question, will it all be in the form of money? Probably not, but the blessing will come in order to meet all your needs and to make you a blessing to others. (Ecclesiastes 11:1; Proverbs 3:7; 11:24, 25)

Rebuke your Enemies: *"And I will rebuke the devourer for your sakes and shall not destroy the fruits of your ground."*

In the agrarian culture the devourer were insects, animals, diseases, floods and draughts that could destroy the crops. For most of us today devourers are materialism, greed, bad spending habits, gluttony, debts, diseases and many others. God will rebuke all these and foes that devour our finances, even diseases. May God deliver you from devourers and surprise your enemies!

Restore your fruitfulness: *"neither shall your vine cast her fruits before the time in the field says the Lord of Host. Then all the nations will call you blessed for you will be a land of delight says the Lord of host"*

God makes a promise to protect our income so that no evil comes to us. Through tithing you create a hedge around you and your family. Remember, Job 1:10 Satan tells God about Job *"have you not made a hedge around him, around his household, and around all that he has on every side? You have blessed the work of his hands and his possessions have increased in the land."* Now that is what God will do to a faithful man or woman who obeys the decrees of the Lord to *"bring all your tithes to the storehouse..."* May the Lord build a hedge around you!

CHAPTER FIVE

SCRIPTURAL BASIS OF TITHING:

Many people misunderstand the purpose of tithe. Others have ignored it as insignificant. Whatever God does have a great meaning and the meaning is seen in the fulfillment. Some people say that tithe is a part of the Law and we are living during the time of grace. That is not true! Abraham who lived before the Law gave a tithe to Melchizedek (Gen. 14:20). Jacob promised to give a tithe to God in Gen 28:22. Tithe is not a part of the law, it is a principle established by God for the benefit of His people.

Tithing goes back to the garden where God reserved something for himself. Adam was given to eat all the trees of the garden except one. This is a picture of the tithe. The first murder was committed over tithing. *"Abel also brought off the first fruit of his flock and of their fat. And the Lord respected Abel and his offering"* **Gen. 4:4.** Many people mistakenly believe that Abel's offering was accepted because it involved the shedding of blood. Abel's sacrifice was accepted because it complied with the principle of tithing and it was offered by faith. It was the first fruit and the best. God accepted the first fruit of other things other than animals and He still does. So Cain's offerings were not accepted, not because it lacked blood but the principle was not right. The scripture is very clear *"Cain brought an offering of the fruit of the ground to the Lord"* **Gen. 4:3** He brought the fruit of the ground but Abel did not just bring the first fruit of his flock but the first born of his flock. Abel observed the principle of tithing and God accepted His offering.

A misunderstanding of the absolute importance of the tithing and its preferred status coupled with ignorance of sound financial management strategies are the primary reasons for financial bondage among Christians today. It is a costly mistake to minimize the importance of the tithe. This practice observed by Adam, Abel,

Abraham and others before the law was codified into the law(Lev.27:30).Malachi the last Prophet of the

The Old Testament written four hundred years before Jesus was born, called people to remember what they had ignored. In the book of Malachi God says *"For I am the Lord, I do not change"* **Mal.3:6.** God never changes. He has not changed his intentions for tithing.

"Will a man rob God? Yet you have robbed me! But you say in which way have we robbed me? In tithes and offerings. You are cursed with a curse, for you have robbed me. Even the whole nation. Bring all your tithes into the storehouse that there may be food in my house. And try me in this "Says the lord of host. "If I will not open for you the windows of heaven and pour out for you such a blessing that there will be room enough to receive it". "And I will rebuke the devourer for your sakes so that he will not destroy the fruits of your ground. Nor shall the vine fail to bear fruits for

you in the field "Says the lord of host. "And all the nations will call you blessed, for you will be a delightful land" Says the lord of host. Mal.3:8-12.

It is clear from this portion of scripture that Israel was neglecting her covenant relationship with God by robbing Him of tithes and Offering. That bought retributive judgment. Now God challenged her to counter her neglect by proving His faithfulness in the matter of giving. If she would give all her tithes He would open the windows of heaven and pour out blessings. Another translation says I will open the "floodgates of heaven". A floodgate releases without limitation. God who never changes is saying by not paying your tithe you rob Him. You may be an intercessor but if you don't pay your tithe you are a robber trying to intercede before God. You may be a minister, Praise and worship leader if you are not paying your tithe you are a robber.

There is a story told of a dying preacher. He sent a message for his banker and his lawyer, both members of his Church, to come to his home. When they came they were ushered up to his bedroom. As they entered the room the preacher held out his hands and motioned for them to sit on each side of the bed. The preacher grasped their hands, sighed contentedly, smiled and stared at the ceiling. For a time no one said anything. Both the banker and the Lawyer were touched and flattered that the preacher would ask them to be with him during his final moments. They were puzzled that the Preacher had never given them any indication that he liked either of them. They both remembered his many uncomfortable sermons about greed, covetousness, tithing and giving that made squirm in their seats. Finally, the Banker said "Preacher why did you ask us to come" The old preacher mustered up his strength and then said weakly "Jesus died between two thieves and that's how I want to go."

All tithes of all things belong to God. You don't offer your tithe to God you pay your tithe. God is asking you to pay your tithe for it is rightfully His. When you have not given it you are keeping what does not belong to you by any means. By not paying your tithe you are imposing a curse in your life. *"You are cursed with a curse for you have robbed me"* **Mal. 3:9.** You ask how I can be a curse. Jesus Christ has redeemed me from the curse of the law. True! The blood of Jesus has set us free from eternal separation with God and through the same blood we are assured of eternal life.

The curse addressed here is a curse of life. You are a born again Christian but if you don't pay your tithe you bring upon yourself a curse of life. God withholds blessing from you. You live with lack and want always trying to make ends meet but with no success. Misfortune, failure and defeat become the order of the day. Sickness and disease become a common occurrence. This is surely a curse! Whatever you gain out of your labor goes to unprofitable means.

"You have sown much and bring in little; you eat but do not have enough; you drink but you are not filled with drink; you clothe yourself but no one is warm; And he who earns wages, earns wages to put into a bag with holes." Thus says the Lord of hosts "consider your ways! Haggai 1:6-7

A curse opens one to all kinds of vulnerabilities. Many people complain to God about their needs but God who never changes says, consider your ways! Fulfill your covenant relationship. You may not die immediately for not paying your tithe but a slow death will come to you in life.

As a child of God you don't become a sinner in the worldly nature for not paying your tithe but it may lead you there. These are the little foxes that you got to be aware lest they destroy the fruits of your vines.

Our obedience and willingness to pay our tithes are the releasers of the floodgate. Therefore, your tithes are the guarantee of your blessing. Your tithe gives God a legal basis to open the windows of heaven. This is a great lesson that every child of God must know.

Unfortunately, teachers are few. Many people don't teach because they are not comfortable with the subject. Others think that people will suspect them of wanting their money and even others don't teach because they are not tithers. Teacher!

If God is comfortable with the tithe you better be comfortable. By not teaching it, you deny your people a great blessing that cannot be substituted with anything else. Don't fear what people say, fear what God says! If you are a tither you have authority to teach.

Many Pastors invite other people to come and talk about it to their congregations. Listen, Servant of God! Whatever you cannot teach to your people no one has the right to teach them. If you are a tither you have the mandate to teach and receive people's tithes. Nothing will keep a wise believer from tithing!

The earth belongs to the Lord and He owns everything in it. We ought to understand that those who live in it must pay the rent.

"The earth is the Lord's and all its fullness; the world and those who dwell therein. For He has founded it upon the seas and established it upon the waters"

The earth belongs to God who created it and sustains it and that He charges rent to every person since every person derives both sustenance and wealth from the earth. This rent is equal for every person. It never changes; it remains Ten percent of the person's increase. Those for whatever reasons do not pay their tithes, have that amount or more stolen from them by the devourer. The reason for God choosing the tithe to be paid is so that it can support His ministry.

Numbers 18:21 *"Behold I have the children of Levi all the tithe in Israel as an inheritance in return for the work which they perform, the work of the tabernacle of meeting"* The tithe is God's way of supplying for the ministry. Throughout the Bible God has indicated the importance of the tithes. *"And all the tithe of the land, whether of the seed of the land or the fruit of the tree, is the Lord's; it is holy to the LORD" Leviticus 27:30.*

God intended that those who were called to the work of the ministry should not be involved in business enterprises or normal work activities in which others would be involved. Instead they had to totally involve themselves with the service of the Lord. The Levites who were of Aaron's descent were to serve as priests; all other Levites served as assistant Priests. They did not have land as an inheritance lest they abandon their responsibilities of serving God to go farming. It is not God's intention that those who serve him do other jobs. He wants His servants to devote all their time in His service. Many servants of God are involved in other economic activities because things have changed. In the Bible days worship was centralized. All people came to worship in one place. All Israel brought their tithes to one central place. It was therefore possible for the priest to share in what was brought to the tabernacle. The dynamics today are different but the principle remains. Today we worship in many different places and also as different organizations and assemblies. Some of the assemblies are not able to meet their minister's needs and so many ministers have secular jobs to be able to meet their basic needs. Now this is not the intention of God. Apostle Paul taught that a minister of the Gospel should live on the Gospel. People should give to the ministry so that there is enough for the minister and the ministry. This will make the minister put hundred percent effort into the service of God.

When God said that people should pay their tithe of all things He wanted His servant not to lack anything. He did not want people to have more than His servants. He wanted them to have what people have. If it is livestock His servant should have livestock, if it is cereals his servant have cereals, if it is oil they have plenty of oil. To be honest to the scriptures, God intended that the servant to have more than individual members of the congregation, so that no individual could corrupt the minister or the ministry of God through their wealth. Notice in the Old Testament it was one tribe that was provided for by eleven tribes. They were to receive to the ratio of 11:1; God said He is their inheritance.

When a minister seeks another employment because his congregation is not paying their full tithe, God is not happy with that congregation and they are under a curse (Malachi 3:8, 11). After Nehemiah had completed building the wall of Jerusalem he set everything in order and went back to Shushan. After sometime he came back only to find that the services of God had stopped. He says

"I also realized that the portions for Levites (tithe), had not been given to them; for each of the Levites and singers who did the work had gone back to their fields" **Nehemiah 13:10.**

The work of God flourishes and grows when people obey God's principle of providing for His ministry. But with violation of the principle comes a curse, lack of blessing and ultimately a fall.

Jesus in the New Testament did not condemn tithe but rather approved it. ***"Do not think that I come to abolish the law or the prophets; I have not come to abolish them but to fulfill them"*** **Matthew 5:17.**

Jesus did not come to do away with the law but He came to clarify it, He came to make it simple. Tithe has never been abrogated or abolished.

The purpose of tithing and offering is:

- To learn to always fear, revere and honor God. ***"Be sure to set aside a tenth ...that you may learn to revere the Lord your God always"*** **Deuteronomy 14:22,23**

- To establish a reminder of God's ownership. *"Everything comes from you and we have given you only what comes from your hand"* **1 Chronicles 29:14**

- Tithing is external evidence of an internal commitment. It is an expression of an inward attitude.

- To support the ministry and outreach of a local church.

"He ordered the people living in Jerusalem to give the portion due to priests and the Levites so they could devote themselves to the law of the Lord. As soon as the order went out the Israelites generously gave the first fruits of their grains; new wine, oil and honey and all that the field produced. They brought a great amount of tithe of everything"

2Chronicles 31:4,5

The support of the ministry begins with the minister. Some people believe that if the minister has enough he will not pray for the ministry. So they starve him so that he can always pray. When he is starving he will be asking God to remove the starvation and guess who will bear the blunt, those who are withholding their tithes in order to persecute his servant. Jesus would not minister where people refuse to give. The Lord himself said **"It is more blessed to give than to receive" Acts 20:35.**

The religious ideas that equate the ministry with poverty and constant financial struggle are a far cry from the scriptures. Poverty and holiness are not bedfellows. Many servants of God called into the fivefold ministry have been forced to take secular jobs in order to provide for their financial obligations while trying to carry on the ministry as best as they could.

I believe God designed the ministry to be self sustaining, so that those called could give themselves fully to prayer and the ministry of the word.(Though this is my personal opinion).

DON'T BE MISLED:

A tithe is the ten percent of your total income. The Bible says it must be the first and the best. You don't give a tithe, you pay a tithe, it belongs to God. *"Every other offering answers to the earth, but tithe answers in heaven. Tithe has a heavenly transaction link which guarantees you the opening of the windows of heaven."* **David Oyedepo.**

Tithe is an obligation for all believers. It is God's way of supporting the ministry and believers must support God in doing so. You are to pay your tithe in the house of God. In the Bible days they took their tithes and offering to the tabernacle.

Today the tabernacle is the Church. We bring our tithes to the Church. *"But you shall seek the place where the*

Lord your God chooses out of all your tribes to put His name for His dwelling place: and there you shall go. There you shall take your burnt offerings, your sacrifices, your tithes, the heave offerings of your hand, your vowed offerings, your freewill offerings and the firstborn of your herds and flocks." **Deuteronomy 12:5, 6**

You don't take your tithe everywhere. There is a place chosen by God and that is in your local Church. This is the place where you are spiritually nourished and your spiritual needs are met. Therefore, that is where you pay your tithe. Your tithes and those of others take care of the ministers and other needs of the Church.

They keep the ministry of God going on. Some people pay their tithes to ministries of their choice and not in their local church. And even others pay tithe to themselves. That is against God's order; your tithes belong to God and to His house.

If your spiritual needs are met in that ministry you owe them your tithes but if you are a member of a local church giving your tithe to another ministry, you are robbing both God and the local church you belong to.

Remember, that is where you go for counseling, that is where you take your children for dedication and other ministries. Your tithes belong there!

It is good to support Evangelistic ministries and others for the sake of Kingdom expansion but not with our tithes. We can support them with our love offerings. When we break a covenant principle we stop the intended results.

We are living in a time when people don't fear God anymore. There are so many so-called Bishops, Prophets and Pastors who do not have any congregation yet they go around collecting tithes from ignorant members of local churches. They prey on the foolish flock.

"My people perish for lack of knowledge" **Hosea 4:6.** Tithe is given to the Priests for their performance. If

someone is not performing he does not deserve to receive tithes of the people.

"Behold I have given the children of Levi all the tithes in Israel as an inheritance in return for the work

which they perform, the work of the tabernacle of meeting" **Numbers 18:21.**

In the New Testament this idea is brought out by Apostle Paul. *"Let the elders who rule well be counted worthy of double honor especially those who labor in the word and doctrine. For the scripture say you shall not muzzle an ox while it treads out the grain and the laborer is worthy his wages"* **1 Timothy 5:17, 18.**

Any Elder (minister) who is not performing and ruling well in his ministry does not deserve to be rewarded. But those who perform and rule well deserve a double honor.

Every believer must pay their tithe regardless of their status in the ministry. The Pastor is first a believer before he can be a Pastor. He must pay his or her tithe. Many Pastors argue that because they have given themselves to the ministry they are exempted. No one is exempted from paying the tithe. *" Speak thus to the Levites and say to them: when you take from the children of Israel the tithes which I have given you from them as your inheritance, then you shall offer up a heave offering of it to the Lord, a tenth of the tithe"* **Numbers 18:26**. When you receive from the congregation of their tithes and offerings you shall give a tenth of their tithes to the Lord.

CHAPTER SIX.

TEN REASONS WHY YOU SHOULD PAY YOUR TITHE:
Whatever you do should be backed by reason and understanding from the word of God. Here are ten reasons why you should pay your tithe.

REASON 1: TITHE BELONGS TO GOD.

"A tithe of everything from land, whether grains from the soil or fruit trees belong to the Lord; it is holy to the Lord" **Leviticus 27:30.**

The tithe of everything belongs to God. In the hands of a sinner or a saint it belongs to God. It is holy unto the Lord. Is that a true doctrine? Let us see what the scripture says. *"The earth is the Lord's and all its fullness; the world and those who dwell therein"* **Psalm 24:1.** So both the believer and unbeliever and all they possess belong to God. Their tithes belong to GOD.

Abraham gave a tithe to Melkizedeck who was a type of Christ **(Genesis 14:18; Hebrews 7:1-10).** Jacob on his way to his uncle Laban to look for a wife he came to Bethel. The night fell and he slept there. In the morning he made a vow to God. One of the things included in the vow was a tithe. *"And this stone which I have set as a pillar shall be God's house, and all that you give me I will surely give a tenth to you"* **Genesis 28:22.** He vowed to give his tithe to God because it belongs to Him.

The tithe, although found in later Mosaic Law, originated with earlier Patriarchs. Therefore, the tithe is a part of Abrahamic covenant of grace not merely of the Mosaic covenant of works.

Because tithe belongs to God, it must be the first and the best. *"All the best of oil, all the best of the new wine, and grain, the first fruits which they offer to the Lord, I have given them to* you"**Numbers 18:12.** *"Of all your gifts you shall offer up every heave offering due to the Lord from all the best of them, the sanctified part of them"* **Numbers 18:29.**

In establishing the tithe and its regulations God established where the tithe should be given. *"But you shall seek the place where the Lord your God chooses, out of all your tribes, to put his name for his dwelling place and there you shall go. There you shall take your burnt offerings, your sacrifices, your tithes, the heave offerings of your hands, your vowed offerings, your free will offerings and the firstborn of your herds and flocks"* **Deuteronomy 12:5,6.**

The tithe is not given everywhere or anywhere. There is a place for it and that is the place which the Lord your God has chosen for you. This is the place where your spiritual needs are met, where you are fed with the word of God, where you are prayed for and where all other ministries are given to you. This is what Prophet Malachi calls the storehouse. It is the storehouse where all your blessings are stored. From the time of Hezekiah there was a storehouse for deposition of tithes and offerings. The New Testament counterpart to the storehouse is the local Church. This is where you take your children for dedication. If you are a member of a local church that is the place the Lord your God has chosen for you a

and that is where you take your tithes and offerings. If you give your tithes elsewhere you are robbing both that church and God.

Many people pay their tithe to ministries of their choice and not in their local church. This is against God's order and principle. Your tithes belong to your local church. Whenever you have a spiritual need or crisis in your life you go to your Pastor. It would be robbing him of his rightful support when you pay your tithe elsewhere. It is good to give to evangelistic ministries but be sure to give tithes to the storehouse; the chosen place is your local church. A biblical blessing is a result of a biblical principle applied.

Psalm 24:1 says the earth is the Lord's. Those who use lands or buildings belonging to others are expected to pay rent to lawful owners; therefore, those who use

God's earth and resources owe God, the lawful owner's rent. The tithe is the rent money and therefore any person not just the believer, anyone who does not pay is a thief and a robber. The tithe is an acknowledgement of God's ownership and our stewardship. The tithe is not just a bit of ancient legalism; it is a confession of faith wrought indeed rather than words.

REASON TWO: TITHE IS GOD'S WAY OF SUPPORTING THE MINISTRY:

"Behold, I have given the children of Levi all the tithes in Israel as an inheritance in return for the work which they perform the work of the tabernacle of meeting" **Numbers 18:2.**

The support of the ministry begins by supporting his servants or ministers. There can never be a ministry without a minister. All ministries begin with God appointing or calling one into the ministry. When God calls he assigns and when He assigns He provides. From the pages of the Old Testament we see God setting up a strategy for supporting the ministry by asking every Israelite to give their tithes. *"Behold I have given the children of Levi all the tithes in Israel as an inheritance in return for the work which they perform the work of the tabernacle of meeting"* **Numbers 18:2**.

God intended that those who were called to the ministry should not be involved in business enterprises or the normal work activities in which others would be involved. Instead, they were to be totally devoted to serving the Lord.

By not paying your tithes you are conspiring with the enemy on how to defeat God's work. Some people believe since the New Testament believers are called to be kings and priests, should not pay their tithe. God makes no distinction between those whom He has called into the fivefold ministry and other believers.

Throughout the Old Testament God had people whom He called specially to give service to him. This included the ministries of Priests, Levites and Prophets. In the New Testament it is comprised of Apostles, Prophets, Evangelists, Pastors and Teachers. It is God who calls them and anoints them for the ministry. In order for the work of God to continue with an impact the Ministers need to be fully supported. Some people who are selfish have said that if the Minister has more he will not continue to pray for his people.

Some have even starved their pastors so that he can be humble. This is not godly and does not please God. Note, there were eleven tribes in Israel that gave to one tribe. They were commanded to give the first and the best. Now watch, when eleven tribes gave their tithes each, the Levites had eleven tithes. In essence the Levites had one hundred and ten percent (although it was given individually by every member of the tribe).

After they gave their tithes they were left with more than the rest of the tribes. They had the best the land could produce, the best of livestock, the best of oil and wine, the best of everything because that is what people were required to give.

The logic behind this is that they be one step ahead of other people so that no one could corrupt them with material things or compromise them not to say what the Lord has commanded them to say or do.

Many who have been called to the fivefold ministry have experienced the frustration of having to involve themselves in secular work in order to provide financial support while trying to carry on the ministry as best as they could.

Jesus said **"You cannot serve two masters you will either please one or annoy the other"** God's way to support His ministry is through the giving of His people. As a Church, when your pastor takes on a secular job in order to support himself and his family as he serves you, that is a tragedy! Your blessings will be held by God because of not providing for your Pastor through your tithes and offerings.

Once a Pastor gave a testimony in our Church and said "There was a couple in his Church who paid their tithes faithfully. The husband worked in the city so most of the time he gave the tithe to his wife to take to Church. One time the wife saw a very good sweater. She admired it but she did not have the money except the tithe. She went ahead and bought it with the tithe's money. From there she did not take the tithe to the church whenever it was given to her by the husband but used it for her own purposes. She did not tell her husband what she was doing. She became pregnant and after sometime she could not understand this pregnancy.

After nine months there was no delivery, after one year there was nothing and it became a big concern for the family. They went to the Pastor for prayers and advice.

After enquiring how long the pregnancy was the Pastor asked them about their walk with the Lord and they said they were in right standing. He asked them "How about your tithe? The man said "I give to my wife every end month"

At this point the wife interjected as she sobbed with tears falling from her eyes "I have not been bringing". The husband was shocked and became very angry with his wife. The Pastor cooled the man down. The wife said that she became pregnant immediately so she bought the sweater. She repented and the Pastor prayed for her. During prayer her pregnancy disappeared and she was not pregnant any more. She had carried a curse for all that time.

Many people carry within themselves curses of unfaithfulness and disobedience for lack of paying their tithes. They try to work hard but it seems fruitless.
When they get money they cannot see what they have done with it.

"You looked for much but indeed it came to little; and when you brought it home I blew it away. Why?" Says the Lord of hosts "Because of my house that is in ruins, while every one of you runs to his own house" **Haggai 1: 9.**

God is addressing the issue of supporting His ministry which many had denied. Tithe is God's plan of supporting His ministry.

REASON THREE: IT IS A COMMAND OF THE LORD:

"Bring all your tithes in the storehouse that there may be food in my house. And try me in this" says the Lord of hosts "If I will not open for you the windows of heaven and pour out for you such blessings that there will not be room enough to receive it" **Malachi 3:10.**

Your obedience in paying your tithe proves God opens the windows of heaven to you. Reading from verses 8-12 it comes out very clearly God's prosperity plan includes tithing. Many people are handicapped by their own poverty, and too often their poverty is caused by their disobedience to the word of God. This passage clearly tells us that those who withhold their tithes and offerings are robbing God. As a result they are also robbing themselves of the blessings that God wants to bestow upon them. Here God calls us to bring our tithes in return He promises abundance. It is a command of the Lord that we bring our tithes failure to which we become robbers to God. Your obedience and willingness to pay your tithe are the releasers of the floodgates of heavens. Your tithe gives God a legal basis to open the windows of heaven for you.

*"I will rebuke the devourer for your sakes so that he will not destroy the fruit of your ground nor shall the vine fail to bear fruit for you in the field, Says the Lord of Host."***Malachi 3:11**

Your tithe becomes a key to the protection and sustainability of your possessions. God is actually saying, if you are faithful in your tithes He will not allow any destroyer.

What God did in the olden days He still does today! **Malachi 3:6 "I am the Lord I do not change..."**He never changes what he commanded still stands, consider your ways. God's children will hear His voice and obey. Jesus said **"My sheep hear my voice."** If you belong to Jesus you will obey his command.

Any other offering you give is according to what God has blessed you. But this one is clearly defined as **"Bring all your tithes**..." it's a command. Tithing is your God-given privilege to establish your destiny of prosperity.

REASON FOUR: TITHE IS A FAVOR FROM GOD (Malachi 3:10)

In fulfilling this great covenant principle God releases His favor upon you. *"I will open for you the windows of heaven; and pour out for you such blessing that there will not be room enough to receive it"*

Those who fulfill this will receive a great favor of overflowing blessings. You can experience the windows of heavens actually opening with blessings you cannot be able to contain. It is a favor because God promises to rebuke the devourer for your sakes. He will cause every blessing that has your name written on it to be directed to you and Satan himself cannot stop it. This is a favor from God!

Jesus could not minister where people refuse to give. He will not release the favor and grace of any kind for he said *"It is more blessed to give than to receive."* **Acts 20:35**

Tithe attracts favor from God. Note, it is not paying for one or few months that releases favor but it is a continuous process in your life. Remember, when you commit yourself to the heavenly demands the heavens will be committed to your personal demands. Please understand that paying of your tithes does not enrich

God. It is in order for you to secure your covenant destiny with Him. Every other offering answer on earth but tithe answers in heaven. Tithe has a heavenly transaction link which guarantees you the opening of the windows of heaven. Tithe is your God-given privilege to establish your destiny of prosperity against the wicked arrows of life.

"And I will rebuke the devourer for your sake and he shall not destroy fruit or your ground; neither shall your vine cast her grapes before the time in the field says the Lord of Host" **Malachi 3:11**

God promises to open the windows of heaven when you obey this covenant obligation. The windows of heaven remain shut as long as you disobey God's command. By your tithe you give God a legal basis to open the windows of heaven. There is something worth noting in Malachi 3:10, 11. Twice God has said *"I will open the windows of heaven"* *"I will rebuke the devourer"*

Anytime the phrase I will appear in the scriptures spoken by God, it shows His commitment and determination in what He is about to do. It also shows favor or displeasure to the recipient. In this text God shows His favor to the tither which results in their wellbeing, success and prosperity. Remember! God is never mocked because He is true to His word. It is a favor from God!

There are four rewards of tithing found in Malachi Chapter 3:

1. There will be no lack of money to carry out the administration of the local Church and for the completion of the Great Commission.

2. There will be an opening of the windows of heaven. How widely the windows will open is based entirely upon your generosity. You establish the measure of the flow of blessings, successes and prosperity from the floodgates.

3. There will be recognition from unbelievers of the Lord's blessings.

REASON FIVE:IT IS AN EXPRESSION OF THANKS GIVING. (Deuteronomy 14:22, 23; 1 Chronicles 29:14)

The purpose of tithing is to always learn to fear, revere and honor the Lord God. *"Be sure to set aside a tenth....that you may learn to revere the Lord your God always"* **(Deut. 14:22, 23)** It keeps you reminded of God's ownership. In paying of your tithe you express the inward attitude. It is an acknowledgement of the

greater providence of God. If we love God we shall express our love to Him. **1Chronicles 29:14** *"Everything comes from you and we have given you only what comes from your hands"* It's an inward expression of an outward attitude. Remember! Your attitude determines your altitude!

In our thanksgiving we share with God what he has already given to us. It is a recognition of God's enablement on our part in order to have what we have. He has given meaning to our labor by giving it productivity.

Malachi 3:10 *"Bring the entire tithe into the storehouse. That there may be food in my house. And try me in this"* says the Lord of Host. *"If I will not open for you the windows of heaven and pour out for you such a blessing. That there will be no room enough to receive"*

There is something worthy to note in this passage. When the word 'I will' appears in the Bible, it shows God's His commitment and determination in what He is about to do.

It shows the favor of God to the recipient. In this case God shows his favor to the tither, which results in their wellbeing, success and prosperity.

If the Bible teaches us anything about our responsibility to the Lord and His work it is in tithing. It teaches that ten percent of our income is the basis of our giving to

God. Actually, until we have tithed, we do not give God anything. Giving begins after tithing. Tithing is therefore an expression of gratitude and thanksgiving for all that God has given.

We live in a consumer oriented society and we are manipulated by advertisers to always feel we are lacking and so we need more.

Prov. 30:15-16. *"The leech has two daughters. Give and Give! There are three things that are never satisfied. Four, never say "Enough" The grave, the barren womb, the earth that is not satisfied with water- And the fire never says "Enough"*

From time in memorial a growing greed is forever present,

because of our sinful and selfish natures. We all have a materialistic appetite of a blood sucking leech. We are never satisfied with what we have. Nothing is ever enough, we want more and more.

Many people live like the two daughters of Mrs. Leech. Their heart's cry is a growing crescendo of give me, give me and give me. They go through life as takers rather than givers as consumers rather than sharers as leech rather than lovers! Lovers give while leeches take. Leeches bloat themselves with the blood of their victims. Materialism sucks the blood of our spiritual lives.

As a result we are left with diseases of self: Selfishness, Self-centeredness, Self-seeking, Self-satisfaction, Self-indulgence, Self-reliance, and Self-deception. The result of this is that our thankfulness, love, compassion, caring and giving becomes anemic, weak or nonexistent. We need to ask ourselves soul searching questions.

Am I a leech or a lover?

Am I a taker or a giver?

Am I a pillar or a Caterpillar?

Do I live to get or live to give?

God knew his people could be overtaken by the spirit of greed and become thankless so He gave those feasts and sacrifices. One was offering and thanksgiving (Leviticus 7:12, 13, 15; 22:29; Psa.50:12 etc). This was a tangible way of reminding them to be constantly thankful before God. Tithe is an expression of our thankfulness to the Almighty God.

REASON SIX: TITHE IS AN ACT OF WORSHIP TO GOD.

Tithe is an acknowledgement of God's ownership and our stewardship. Tithe is not just a bit of ancient legalism, it is a confession of faith wrought in deeds rather than in words. More than paying the debt, tithing is a form of worship. It is a practice that relate to divine truth to one's daily living for man is obligated to give God at least a tithe of his income.

More than an obligation, tithing is a glorious and happy privilege. In doing so you share in the great work of redemption. This is a ministry in which not even the angels in heaven can participate.

Exodus 23:25 *"Worship the Lord your God and His blessing will be on your food and water. I will take away sicknesses among you" Our* worship through tithing results in our protection and safety. **Malachi 3:11** *"And I will rebuke the devourer for your sakes. So that he will not destroy the fruit of your ground. Nor shall your vines fail to bear fruit for you in the field" says the Lord of Host.*

Tithe insures you against all evils and attacks from the enemy and increases the fruit of your ground. Worship God with your first fruit and the best and you shall live in the comfort of His protection.

In the Old Testament God commanded people to go to Jerusalem for worship! One of the things they had to bring with them was their tithes. Requiring the people to take time off and travel as a family to Jerusalem had several positive results. Among other things, it helped the man to keep his priorities in order. While work was important, it was never permitted to override the importance of a man's worship and his relationship with his family.

Tithe and worship are so connected that it is difficult to separate them. Those who love God obey His instructions and give worship to Him. You cannot worship God and not obey Him. Paying of the tithe is obedience to God's instruction. Obedience is the key to worship. Tithe is an act of worship.

Remember! Abraham when he was instructed by God to offer his Isaac his Son as a sacrifice. Abraham saw it as worship to God. **Genesis 22:5 *"And Abraham said to the young men "stay here with the donkey the lad and I will go yonder and worship and we will come back to you"*** What a faith! No wonder he was called a friend of God!

REASON SEVEN: TITHE IS A THERMOMETER OF OUR FAITH IN GOD.

If you love God you will obey Him and you will give all to Him. When you have faith in God you will have no problem in giving Him what he requires. Paying of your tithe demonstrates your faith in God. It is through paying of our tithes that we break the spirit of greed.

The only sure way of giving to God is by giving into His ministry, for the ministry is the only agency authorized by God to receive tithes and offering in His name. Every revival in the scriptures was preceded by an act of obedience in paying the tithes and restoration of the Priests and Levites. Whenever people had faith in God they brought their tithes of all things; of livestock and of crops to the storehouse. They brought the first and the best.

Tithing equates to making a sacrifice. For the past 2000 years plus, the rendering of tithes and offering to the Lord is the closest thing to sacrificing. When you offer money to the Lord, you give yourself to him since you have exchanged a part of your life for money.

The money you offer to God represents your life. Our faith in God is demonstrated by our deeds. Abraham offered his son Isaac a sacrifice to God.

In the Old Testament tithe was a physical and visible material symbol of the people's humility and reverence to God. It demonstrated the giver's faith and love for God. Many Christians give sporadically some kind of offering to God they do not constantly tithe.

Many Christians **Tip** but they do not tithe. In a very real sense a tithe is an indicator of the level of our love and commitment for God. The tithe can be thought of as the currency of the heart. *Remember! The number one competitor in your life to the Lordship of Christ is MONEY! Money is a master as Christ is a master. "No servant can serve two masters...... You cannot serve both God and money (LUKE 16:13) Therefore, either*

Christ will be your master or money will be your master!

Your money more than anything else reveals the true treasure of your heart! Giving is a tangible physical indicator of your true spiritual condition. How you spend your time and how you spend your money will impact your eternity more than anything else. When it comes to money and materialism there is more of the **"world in the Church"** than there is **"Church in the world".**

Too many Christians mirror and reflect the economic greed of the world rather than the economic contentment that is supposed to characterize God's people.

REASON EIGHT: IT IS AN ACT OF JOY TO PAY MY TITHE

After one has worked for a period of time he is rewarded with a payment. A farmer having worked in his farm receives a harvest. It is a time of joy and jubilation when one takes the harvest. Tithing is an expression of this joy. It is recognition that God is the giver of the harvest.

Deut.8:18 "And *you shall* **remember the Lord your God for it is He who gives you power to get wealth; that He may establish His covenant which He sore to your fathers, as it is this day"**

It is God who gives the ability, means, endurance and capacity to obtain wealth, for material blessings are included in the promises given to the Patriarchs and their descendants. One can be tempted to think that it is his knowledge, skills and ability which has given him what he has. Without God's ability one can do nothing. Paying of our tithes brings us to appreciate what God has given to us. And we are able to say we have nothing unless it is given to us by you.

In the olden days of the Temple people brought the first fruits of their produce with joy, singing and dancing. It was a great celebration recorded in Leviticus 23:9-14. Remember, the Apostle Paul's words **2Cor. 9:7** *"for God loves a cheerful giver"* For thirty days God has given you good health and strength to work. With your tithe you express your joy to God through paying your tithe. You have invested your money and time in a business and the Lord has given you profit. You should not take it for granted. *"I am the Lord your God who teaches your hands to profit. Who leads you by the way you should go"* **Isaiah 48:17** There are many people who invest and lose and walk away with huge debts but God gave you a profit out of your investment. Your tithe is a joy and gratitude. *"Those who sow in tears will r4eap with songs and joy. He who goes out weeping carrying seeds to sow, will return with songs of joy, carrying sheaves with him"* **Psa. 126:5-6**

REASON NINE: IT IS A CHALLENGE TO PROOF GOD: MALACHI 3:10

Tithing is a part of a timeless covenant that guarantees countless benefits.

"Bring all the tithes into the storehouse, that there may be food in my house and try me in this" **says the Lord of hosts.**

Biblical results come from adhering to biblical principles. God has established a principle of tithe. This principle has unfailing results. God says try me in this, in other words He says proof me in this and see what I will do. He poses a challenge to us to dare Him in paying our tithes.

He promises to open the windows of heaven and release blessings that we cannot contain. **First** when you tithe there will be food in God's house. God's work will advance because there are resources. **Secondly, those** who give will be placed in a position to receive great, overflowing blessings.

The blessings that come by tithe are not always material blessings. They come in many forms; healing, victory in life, breakthrough, success, joy and satisfaction in life.

Tithing is accepting God's challenge that He lays before his people. He has dropped the financial grant by saying **"Test me in this"** Tithing is the spiritual and financial **"key of obedience"** that will open up the floodgates of heaven so that God will be able to pour out so much blessing you will not have room enough for it. Lack of tithing is lack of trusting God. When you are not paying your tithes you are guilty of robbing God but in reality you are guilty of robbing yourself. By not paying your tithe you are taking yourself out from under the blessing of the Lord and placing yourself under the discipline of the Lord by closing the floodgates of heaven to your life! By not taking the challenge to prove God in giving your tithe you are the Big loser not God! He owns it all anyway.

REASON TEN: TITHE IS A PROTECTION COVER: MALACHI 3:11

"And I will rebuke the devourer for your sake, so that he will not destroy the fruit of your ground .Nor shall the vine fail to bear fruit for you in the field" Says the Lord of hosts.

The only way Christians are ever going to break the yoke of debt and lack is by honoring God with their first and the best which is their tithe. This will give God a reason to rebuke the devourer. Paying your tithe willingly and faithfully is entering into a cover covenant where God covers you from the devourer.

Tithing does not only guarantee you a blessing, it also establishes insurance cover against the wicked arrows of life. It is a master key to prosperity. You can have much but the much you have may not help you or satisfy you because the hand of God is not upon it. **Prov. 13:7** *"There is one who makes himself rich, yet has nothing; And one who makes himself poor yet has great riches"* When there is a covering of God upon you, whatever you gather is protected and is useful for you and your family. Your efforts without God are nothing. They are fruitless and result in frustrations.

Haggai 1:5-7 *"Now therefore thus says the Lord of host "Consider your ways" "You have sow much, and bring in little; you eat, but do not have enough; you drink but are not filled with drink; you clothe yourself, but no one is warm; and he who ears wages, earns wages to put into a bag with holes"*

When you don't pay your tithes you place yourself in a position of a curse. Your tithes are a cover upon possessions. After paying ten percent God makes sure that your 90% gives you value. It becomes profitable and is able to meet your needs. The Lord covers you from destruction of your possessions.

A story is told of a Youngman who told his Pastor he had promised God a tithe of his income. They prayed for God to bless his career. At that time he was making $40 a week and tithing $4. In a few years his income Increased and was tithing $500 per week. He called the Pastor to see if he can be released from the promise. It was too costly. The Pastor replied "I don't see how you can be released from your promise but we can ask

God to reduce your income to $40 a week then you would have no problem tithing $4. Give according to your income, lest God make your income according to your giving! Our God is not a respecter of persons, therefore, He instituted tithe so that everyone is treated equally.

CHAPTER SEVEN.

OFFERINGS

An offering is a freewill gift offered to God. It is given cheerfully, willingly and with a clean heart. God rewards unselfish giving to those in need with boundless liberality

. " **Give it will be given to you good measure, pressed down, shaken together, and running over will men give unto your bosom for with the same measure you use, it will be measured back to you."Luke 6:38** Note when Jesus says **"Give"** He also says **"and it will be given to you."**

Giving and receiving belong together. Only when we give are we in a position to expect to reach out and receive a harvest. Jesus said the harvest will be **"good measure, pressed down, shaken together and running over"**

We give as to God and we receive as from God but we should remain sensitive at all times to the different

ways in which God may deliver our harvest. Note!

A miracle is either coming towards you or going past you all the time. Do not let it pass.

There is what is called the law of divine reciprocity. You give, God gives in return. When you plant a seed the ground yields a harvest. That is a reciprocal relationship. The ground can only give to you as you give to the ground. You put money in the bank and the bank returns with interest. That is reciprocity.

Many people want something for nothing when it comes to the things of God. They know that it does not work like that in the world systems, yet they expect God to send them something when they have not invested in His kingdom. If you are not investing your time, talent, commitment and your money, why do you want something? How can you get something when you have not planted any seed? How can you expect God to honor your desire when you have not honored his command to give? Prosperity begins with investment.

God introduced offering so that one can recognize that he has nothing unless it be given by God.

There are various types of giving:

Kingdom Promotion Giving:
This includes freewill offerings which you bring into the house of God every time you come for worship. Never go before the Lord your God empty hands. It is an abuse of privilege. **Deuteronomy 16:16-17,** the instruction was that no one shall appear before the Lord empty handed.

In 1 Corinthians 16:2 "Every man shall give as is able, according to the blessing of the Lord your God which has given you." This is not a tithe it is a freewill offering aimed at promoting the kingdom of God.

The Old Testament has many types of offerings. Some were animal offerings others were cereal offerings and of silver and gold. All these offerings were a constant reminder to the people that God is the giver. Like tithing no one is exempted. Every man shall give as is able. If you are not a giver, no amount of fasting or prayer can save you from being a beggar. Never at any time despite giving.

Proverbs 13:13 "Anyone who despises instructions shall be destroyed." Remember, Jesus said give it shall be given to you. Giving is the way that God wants to increase us, so that we can have abundance in our daily living. Our offerings are for kingdom promotion.

Freewill offering is an appreciation of God's protection and guidance. It is also a thanks giving for the wonderful things He has done. David said **"What shall I render unto the Lord for all his benefits?" Psalm 116:12** Our giving to God demonstrates our attitude toward Him and it shows our character in dealing with material things. The more you are attached to material things the lesser relationship you have with God. Our offerings are a declaration that we are in control of our possession, not the opposite.

Kingdom Demands Giving:

This is a giving that God demands from us for His specific use. **"From what you have, take an offering for the Lord. Everyone who is willing to bring to the Lord an offering of gold, silver and bronze; blue purple and scarlet yarn and fine linen and goat hair; ram skins dyed red, badger skins, and acacia wood; oil for the light and spices for anointing oil and for sweet incense; 'onyx stones, and stones to be set in the ephod and in the breastplate. Exodus 35:4-9.** God demanded this for the building of the Tabernacle. People gave more than what was required. **"And people spoke to Moses saying "the people bring much more than enough for the service of the work which the Lord commanded us to do."Exodus 36:5** When God makes a kingdom demand on you it is so He can add color to your destiny. It is His secret way to promote you. As long as you keep meeting kingdom sacrifices you will never run dry! This is one of the greatest investments, Kingdom investment. Remember! Every investment has dividends. God has made you a steward of His treasures so whenever He needs them you must release them to Him.

Sacrificial Giving:

Nothing turns financial captivity around like sacrifices. Sacrificial giving is when you determine in your own heart to give something to God, not because it is offering time, but because you want God to do something that is so deep in your heart. It is a giving that provokes God's intervention faster in a situation. It is a sacrifice that is so dear to you. Abraham gave sacrifices to God at every juncture of his life and became great. He always gave what was best for him to the Lord. **"And Abraham stretched out his hand and took a knife to slay his son" Genesis 22:10.** It wasn't easy for Abraham but he obeyed and was ready to give that which was so dear to him. This sometimes can be a painful gift which you give to God. But it has great impact. After Abraham gave his son as a sacrifice which he did in his heart though he did not slay him physically, God renewed His covenant with him. **"By myself I have** sworn says the Lord, because you have done this thing, and have not withheld your son, your only son "blessing I will bless you, and multiplying I will multiply your descendants as the stars of heaven and as the send which is on the seashore; and your descendants shall possess the gates of their enemies. In your seed all the nations of the earth shall be blessed, because you have obeyed my voice." Genesis 22:15-18. Every great man you know is a product of his sacrifices.

God honors every sacrifice that is offered to Him with a pure and clean heart. In the third chapter of first Kings Solomon the king of Israel was blessed by God when he sacrificed to Him. The heaven was opened for him as a result of the sacrifices he gave to Him. God gave him beyond what he ever asked.

Giving to the Prophet:

"He that receives a Prophet in the name of a Prophet shall receive a Prophet's reward; and he that receives a righteous man shall receive a righteous man's reward."Matthew 10:41

Prophets are God's anointed messengers sent to be a blessing to us. A minister has power to cause the blessings of God rest a man's life. God has given the Power of attorney to His servant and his word as the words of God.

"Who confirms the word of His servant and performs the counsel of His messenger; who says to Jerusalem you shall be inhabited' to cities of Judah" "you shall be built and I will raise up her waste places." Isaiah.44:26

Prophets are spiritual fathers, so when you touch their hearts you provoke a release of blessing. Giving to the Prophet of God provokes prophetic blessing that cannot be bought with money.

2 Chronicles 20:20 "Jehoshaphat stood and said "Hear me, O Judah and you inhabitants of Jerusalem; Believe in Lord your God and you shall be established, believe in His Prophets and you shall prosper." Prophets of God carry within them the anointing that can turn your life forever. They carry power through the word of God that shapes the destinies of people.

"The Lord used a Prophet to bring Israel up from Egypt; by a Prophet He cared for him" Hosea 12:13. Even today God uses His Prophets to deliver people from their bondage. He uses Prophets to break the yoke of Poverty in people's lives.

The Bible records a story of a widow of Zarephath in **1 Kings 17.** After the brook dried where Elijah was receiving refreshment from the ravens, God sent him to the widow of Zarephath. God said to him **"behold I have commanded a widow in that place to supply you with food."** When the man of God came to that place he saw a woman gathering sticks. **"He called to her and asked** "would you bring me a little water in a jar so I may have a drink?" As she was going to get it he called "and bring me, please a piece of bread" 1 Kings 17:10-11. Remember, this was the time of famine and everyone was careful how they spent whatever little one had.

"As surely as the Lord your God lives" she replied "I don't have any bread only a handful of flour in a jar and a little oil in a jug. I am gathering few sticks to take home and make a meal for myself and my son that we may eat it and die." Elijah said to her "Do not be afraid. Go home and do as you have said. But first make small bread for me, from what you have and bring to me, and then make something for yourself and your son. For this is what the Lord, the God of Israel says: 'The jar of flour will not be used up and the jug of oil will never run dry until the day the gives rain on the land.' She went away and did as Elijah told her. So there was food every day for Elijah and for the woman and her son. For the jar of flour was not used up and the jugs of

oil never run dry in keeping with the word of the Lord spoken by Elijah." 1 Kings 17:12-16.

Note verse 12. The woman had no hope of living after their last meal. She and her son were ready to die. The prophetic brought hope to this family. God provided supernaturally and they were sustained throughout the famine.

It is only a prophetic encounter that can last through your challenges and give you success. Giving to the Prophets grants you access into the prophetic function that they carry. Your life will never run dry! Some of the amazing things in this story are that God had commanded a widow, not a tycoon in Zarephath to supply the Prophet with food. One thing that comes to mind is that this woman must be a rich woman. But it was not so. God looks at what is available and from that, He creates a miracle of multiplication.

This widow had fears of her well being and that of her son. The words of the Prophet ``don't be afraid" dispel all her fears and she gained courage. **Remember! Courage is not the absence of fear but its willingness to hold on and move forward even when you are petrified, fearful and afraid**. The destiny of her family was secured due to her obedience to the word of the Man of God.

Another Prophetic encounter is recorded in 2 Kings 4:8-17, of a woman who recognized a prophet and asked her husband that they build a little chamber where this Man of God could rest while in his mission. This touched the heart of the Man of God and wanted to do something for this woman. The woman said she did not have a need. But the Man of God was not settled. He asked his servant **"what could be done for her?" His servant Gehazi said she has no child and her husband is old. And he said "Call her". And when he had called her, she stood in the door. And he said "About this time next year" Elisha said "you will hold a son in your arms" No my lord" she objected "Don't mislead your servant, O man of God!" But the woman** became pregnant and the next year about that same time she gave birth to a son, just as Elisha had told her." 2 kings 4:14-17.

Have you recognized a Prophet in your life? Taking care of the Prophets, takes care of your cares. When a Prophet speaks a word for you it is bound to come to pass. Remember! Every prophetic blessing lasts forever. Later when her son died she brought her to the Prophet and the Prophet restored his son's life. Whatever comes by a prophetic action is sustained by the same function.

The longing of this woman was satisfied by the prophet. You can provoke prophetic blessing by giving to the Prophets. Prophets are messengers of God sent to every generation. They are agents sent to service the needs of humanity. A Prophet's offering has power to place one above and above only. Honoring a Prophet includes serving him, meeting his need, giving him due respect, praying for him, sowing financial seeds into his life and doing things that will contribute to the success of his divine assignment here on earth.

Giving to the Poor:

The poor around you is an opportunity for your rise in the Kingdom of God.

"He who is kind to the poor lends to the Lord, and will reward him for what he has done" Proverbs 19:17. When you are giving to the poor you are doing that on behalf of God and so you are lending to God. Until you are concerned with the needs of others your needs remain unmet.

"Blessed is he that considereth the poor: the Lord will deliver him in time of trouble. The Lord will preserve him, and keep him alive; and he shall be blessed upon the earth: and thou wilt not deliver him unto the will of his enemies." Psalm 41:1-2 (KJV)

By considering the needy you shall be delivered in time of trouble. Deliverance is far beyond money and possession. It is a combination of all that God can release to the one He favors.

Giving is living! If you are not a giver you are not living. The joy of living is giving. God created us so that we can give. Increase and multiplication is a result of giving. **"Give and it will be given to you a good measure pressed down, shaken together, and running over will be poured into your lap. For with the same measure you use, it will be measured to you." Luke 6:38**

No giver will remain under! "A man's gift makes room for him and brings him before great men." Proverbs 18:16

www.ingramcontent.com/pod-product-compliance
Lightning Source LLC
Chambersburg PA
CBHW060402050426
42449CB00009B/1863